all the things i never said

madison amby

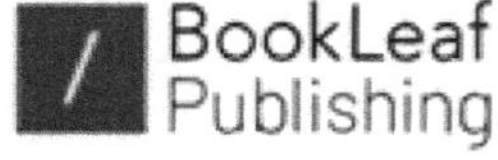
BookLeaf Publishing

Presentation by *BookLeaf Publishing*

Web: www.bookleafpub.com

E-mail: info@bookleafpub.com

ISBN: 9789357211369

First edition 2022

growing up

the three of us walked hand in hand,
and each adventure always felt so grand .
whether that be a walk along the park,
or telling stories in the dark.
through every up and every down we stayed side
by side,
for a beautifully fantastic, and fun filled ride.

you and i

when i close my eyes
there's a little girl playing in a field,
she's beautiful and knows it too,
i watch as she frolics and bounces around,
she is wild and free as one could possibly be.
i watch as she runs and jumps noticing how her
feet lift from the ground so effortlessly with such
grace,
even in a crowded room she makes her presence
known, she takes up space, h holding her head
up high.
her confidence radiates and it makes me smile,
that's when she sees me
her innocent eyes blankly gaze into mine with
such curiosity,
what is she thinking?
does she even recognize me.

we could never talk but this much i know,
she and i saw the world differently.
she saw the sun, the stars, and the light in
everything.
while i saw the darkness and all the many
lurking shadows.

she has yet to see all the horrors hidden just
beneath the surface, and i hope she never does.
but i know she will, the same way i did, and i
want nothing more than to tell her all the things i
wish i heard.

we are a mess but we are a masterpiece

as my eyes slowly open i see the little girl
staring back at me and all i want to do is make
her smile,
i blink ever so slightly and she's gone and i'm
left with nothing but my reflection.

just one more time

in my room I have this shelf.
this shelf that i just can't seem to stop
reorganizing.
no matter how hard i try,
something's not right.

is the clock ticking too slow?
i should reset it.
is the book too far off center?
i should adjust it.
are the flowers wilting?
i should replace them.

every time i look again,
something's still not right.
it's not quite perfect,
yet.

so i start over.
i wipe the shelf clean, i like everything spotless.
i stand the book up tall, she looks proud.
i turn back the clock, now it's right on time.
and i water my flowers, they smell so pretty.
stepping back i still don't like what i see.

what is it this time?
is the clock too fast now?
is the book distracting?
are the flowers too much?
i start over.

an endless cycle of creating and erasing.
i know it has to stop but
is it wrong to demand perfection?
to not ever settle for anything less?
if i want something done, why wouldn't i make
sure it's done right.
"one more time" i tell myself
i tell myself this over and over,
now even i don't believe it.

so i re-pot the flowers, i move the book, and i fix
the clock.
something's still not right.
it's not quite perfect,
yet.

just one more time.

dinner party of two

she's always there
but she typically follows me from a distance.
she'll walk along the other side of the street.
but sometimes,
without warning she'll pick up her pace.
i walk faster hoping she won't keep up,
she's fast i'll give her that.

but why here?
why now?

i cross a few streets and turn few corners,
hoping that i'll lose her.
she's too good.
and before i know it she's right by my side.
i try so hard to ignore her, but she relentlessly
makes herself known.
she makes me so nervous.

99...98...97...96...

i feel myself losing control as i slowly give in to
her
my hands start shaking ever so slightly
but it's the only thing i see.

76…75…74…73…

i'm breathing so heavy ; i watch my chest as it
rises and falls.
wondering why i'm not getting any air,
why am i not getting any air?
i panic.

59…58…57…56

i don't like her here.
i've lost my focus and my visions blurred,
all i see is her.

25…24….23…22

i hear her voice all around me.
it's ringing in my ear.
i'm getting desperate, "stop" i beg
she never listens.

10…9…8…7

she eventually grows tired so she then walks
away,
i'm finally left alone.

3…2…1

relief.

i catch my breath, and dry my tears.
i'm so tired of her,
and i've never liked her company.

she crashes my party,
and ruins my fun.
everywhere i go
she pulls up a seat.

dinner, for party of two:
my anxiety and me.

let me be mad

i'm way too tired of being sad,
so all i ask of you is that you let me be mad.
let me be angry,
for all the things i never said.
for all the feelings have been piling up and it's
getting to my head.

your words, they hurt, they cut so deep.
they taunt me as i try to sleep.
and you don't ever say you're sorry,
you know i hate getting a third party.

i hate the help but know i need it.
but my pride keeps me quiet so all i do is sit.
"real feelings don't just go away", they say, and
it's never been clearer.
especially when the ones you love the most
make you feel so inferior.

i know you love me, i know you care.
so how come you never play fair?
i'm getting tired of defending
the same boundaries and rules you keep on
bending.

i'm always tired but not even sad
all i want to do is be mad.
so let me scream and let me shout,
please just let me get it out.

so then when i wake the next morning,
we can start over without a warning.
a brighter day, a better day,
i wish it could always be this way.

watching the birds

do you ever watch the birds?
notice how they fly together.
having one in the front to lead,
so that the air rushes to the back
giving everyone else the strength and
momentum,
to keep going.

to fly a little higher
for a little longer.

and when the bird begins to bend,
they switch.
but what if she never asks for help,
what if she doesn't want to switch?
what if she doesn't want anyone to see her
falter?
if she doesn't say anything, no one will know.
if she doesn't say anything, no one will see how
hard she's struggling.
they wouldn't have to see her cave,
they'd forever see her as something strong.

the weight of the world is too much for me to
carry,

but please, let me do it on my own.
i want to do it on my own.

i'm slowing down
it's getting bad again,
i know it is.
and i'm moments from throwing the towel in,
having so little left to give.

but i'll stay front and center?
i'll pick up my pace and get things back to
where they used to be,
i just want to fly a little higher for a little longer.

happy birthday

i'm surrounded by all my favorite people,
they're all standing by my side,
their eyes all shining bright and all their smiles
wide.

i watch as we light the candles,
each one representing a year of life it's truly a
beautiful display,
and yet i feels so bittersweet on this melancholy
day.

my mind is filled with memories,
and i cant help but smile,
but deep inside i know this life will only last
awhile.

a tragic thought to say the least, but nothing lasts
forever.
i look up at the ones i love, at least we're here
together.

in this moment

in this moment everything feels perfect,
in this moment everything feels new,
everything's fantastic because i am with you.

your hand wrapped in mine,
our fingers interlocked,
i look into your eyes and it's like the time has
stopped.

the view

say "view" and i'm running the tips of my
fingers across the brick wall lining my backyard.
i'm staring at the sky, amazed with all the puffy
clouds and how lovely they looked with all the
blended colors. a baby blue slowly being
covered by a pink so light and delicate, a
lavender strong but gentle, and an orange bold
and bright. i glance over my shoulder at the boy
who had my entire heart in the palm of his hand.
i told him i loved the view. he looked at me, and
said that his was better.

a beautiful moment that became nothing more
than a distant memory

~ inspired by nikki grimes

our story

when it's all said and done
our story was a slow burn.
a slow burn that went out too quickly after
finally being lit.

after all we've been through
we've done the exact thing we swore we
wouldn't,
we became nothing more than strangers who
knew each other a little too well.

and sometimes
i wonder,
do you ever think of me?
i mean,
does my name ever linger on your lips?
the way that the color of wine would stain,
and the scent would stick.

do certain songs ever remind you of me?
of what we had?
of what you walked away from?

i haven't quite moved on and

maybe it's because you were one of my best
friends, so i'm afraid.
afraid that if i let you go, it means that i've given
up,
given up on you,
given up on us.

or maybe,
just maybe,
holding on to you is just
comfortable.
because maybe it's all i know

you see, i am trying to remember you and let
you go all at the same time.

my take on love

love is a concept, that i just can't get enough of.
i'm in love with the idea of love
and seeing everything it can do.
because love can bring two people with
absolutely nothing in common together, and they
could share a beautiful life together.
but love can also take two people who seemed
absolutely perfect for each other and tear them
apart.

you say love makes people do crazy things, and i
think that's because love itself is absolutely
wild.
a crazy coaster of ups and downs, twists and
turns,
and a million unexpected loops.
a constant cycle of nerves and bliss, fear and
excitement, and everything in between. your
stomachs in a knot and yet,
you never want the ride to end.

my favorite part about this idea of love I've
seemed to conjure up is how there are endless
different types of love, all so different and yet so
similar.

it's the quiet and the chaos, the love that hurts,
and the love that heals. it's this sense of power;
the passion, the patience. it's like standing in the
eye of the storm or flying high above it.

so you see, i have this amazingly incredible idea
of what love is and how it can look,
and yet it feels so out of reach,
unobtainable.

that is until i met you of course.

the intimacy of being
understood

how do you do it? why do you do it?

i want to explain it, i really do.
but the words,
they spill from my lips like a glass one drop too
full,
they entangle themselves into a chaotic ball of
yarn,

and it's all just
so messy.

but you,
you don't seem to mind at all,
you pull up a chair and untangle each section bit
by bit.
regardless of the time spent,
you continue.
regardless of the opportunities missed,
you continue.
you continue until everything is freely lying out
in the open,
as if it were on display.

vulnerability.
such a scary feeling,
and yet you make it feel so safe.

my happy ever after

meeting him was like finding the last golden
ticket.
unexplainable luck, and nothing but pure
excitement.
like finally leaving my tall and cushy tower,
and seeing floating lights for what felt like the
first time in forever.

getting to know him was like reading the exact
story i've always wanted to write.
i let him be a part of my world, and he let me
into his.

all the hours of mindless conversation,
telling him how "i've got a dream'
my hopes, my goals, my secrets,
he listened to it all
he saw all of me for me, and never made me feel
small.

falling for him came so naturally, but it was as if
i were free falling
hoping that i'd never reach the ground.

he is everything i had ever wanted.

everything i could ever ask for and more.
with every penny i've thrown to the bottom of
the fountain,
every wish i've made upon a star,
they're finally granting my wish.

i've learned that a home is not always a roof and
four walls,
because when i click my heels together saying
"there's no place like home."
they bring me straight to him,

he is my safest of places, and yet my biggest
adventure.

if a dream is a wish your heart makes, i guess
my heart asked for him.

a new take

i used to see love as nothing more than a
concept,
something tangible and yet completely
unobtainable.
it was on the highest of shelves, always slightly
out of reach.

love was something that only ever happened on
the big screens,
something many got to witness but very few got
to enjoy.

but you,
you've completely brought this unobtainable
idea to life.
you reached up and brought it right down off it's
shelf, just for me.
you took my heart in the palm of your hand
and held it so gently i couldn't help but smile.

and ever since,
you've shown me the purest love i could ever
possibly imagine,
you've made my life feel like a movie and i
can't seem to stop watching it.

in the story of my life i think you're my favorite
chapter.
i love you oh so very much you're my happy
ever after.

my advice to you

when we spoke last you told me,
"It could be better, but it's good enough."

now i don't know it all but from what i do,
i've written out my advice to you,

find a new definition of what love is
and add it to your dictionary.
rip out any pages of what you thought it was,
and start anew.
because love is not something conditional.
love is not expensive.
and love shouldn't hurt.

and you see, you never see this issue because
you've been walking around with your eyes
closed,
so tight you're able to tune out the rest of the
world and just keep walking.

but please open your eyes,
please stop avoiding all the issues and stop
saying that it's all okay.
you laugh each remark off as if it's funny,

but you know the tears you shed could fill an
entire ocean.

you're staring at the city lights and mistaking
them for stars.
defending those who walk all over you, just for
them to throw you out like trash.

stop defending them.
stop praising them for the bare minimum, just
because you don't believe you deserve anything
more.

you deserve the world,
you deserve the mountains and the seas,
the skies and the stars.
you deserve the world,
the world you keep trying to give others.

heather

to me you are perfect
in all the ways that matter.
and oh what a delight it has been to know you,
and an even greater one to be loved by you.
because your love is unconditional.
your love is everything i thought i never
deserved.
you have seen my highs and my lows,
my bests and my worsts,
and through it all you have never once looked at
me differently.
you have loved me when i've felt unlovable,
you've show me kindness even when i've been
cruel,
you see the beauty in my every flaw and
imperfection,
your love makes me want to love myself.
and my only hope is that i can do the same for
you,
my hope for you is that one day soon you'll see
yourself the way i see you.

a rare beauty

your flawless light that follows you
into every single room,
your kind eyes and gentle heart that make the
flowers bloom,
you are beautiful in every possible way,
and every time we talk it always makes my day.

i know you don't always believe me
but it's so incredibly true,
the world is so much more beautiful
and it's all because of you.

the things you do for others matter

the woman in the market you smiled and gave a
thumbs up to was a single mother balancing two
jobs.
you made her feel seen.

the man you thanked and helped cross the street
was a veteran who lost his sense of sight.
you made him feel appreciated.

the little girl at the mall you complimented had
been trying on dresses all day hating the way she
looked in them.
you made her feel beautiful.

the boy you helped with his homework had been
trying to get his grades up for weeks but was too
nervous to ask for help.
you made him feel heard.

the lady in the hotel you held the door for had
been trying to find a place for her things after
she was forced to leave her home.
you made her feel hopeful.

the guy you sang and danced for in the car next
to you had just been laid off and was trying to
get his mind off of things.
you made him smile.

the woman in the park you called "beautiful"
had been struggling with her physical
appearance for years.
you encouraged her to be kinder to herself.

the coworker you said you were proud of was
feeling unimportant, he was wondering if
anyone would mind him being gone.
you encouraged him to stay.

small acts of kindness save lives.
that's why the things you do for others matter,
no matter how big or small.